Mocktail & Me

BLISS IN EVERY SIP!

QUEENETH ODIMEGWU

Dedicated to Prophetess, Mrs. Veronica Odimegwu

CONTENTS

INTRODUCTION

"People will typically be more enthusiastic where they feel a sense of belonging and see themselves as part of a community, than they will in a place in which each person is left to their own devices"

- Alfie Kohn

Do you remember how excited you felt when you celebrated your favorite team's win, discussed your favorite TV show with a group of fellow fans, marched for a cause you support with a group of people or even dancing to your favorite song in a party? These memorable moments fulfill the need for interconnection and belonging in a way that sitting by yourself in parties, dancing or protesting alone cannot match.

The gleeful feeling you get from the sense of belonging was coined "collective effervescence" by French sociologist Emile Durkheim in his 1912 book "The Elementary forms of Religious life". Durkheim's research focused on religion however, can be applied to all spectrums of life.

The idea of Mocktail & Me stemmed from the idea to promote inclusion in parties and most especially, a sense of belonging - a human need, just like the need for food and shelter. Feeling that your authentic self is welcomed and celebrated contributes to maximizing your full potential. It means you can confidently ask for a non-alcoholic drink at any party without someone raising an eyebrow or causing you to feel "left out".

No one deserves to hide who they really are in order to fit in. Therefore, next time you host a party, learn to diversify the drink menu by including alcoholic and non- alcoholic drinks. When you do that, notice how the party is diversified, inclusivity is promoted and everyone feels a great sense of belonging. Not only that, but everyone is totally happy!

WHAT ARE MOCKTAILS?

While it is known for cocktails, beer and other drinks to complement a meal, the emphasis on non-alcoholic drinks is sometimes overlooked. A mocktail is best described as a non-alcoholic drink with natural fruits, fruit juices as the main ingredients. Additives such as lemon, ginger, sparkling water and herbs can be used to enhance the flavor. Generally mocktails are made and best enjoyed fresh as opposed to storing and pouring from a fountain or pitcher - although there can be exceptions.

Mocktails are often recommended for designated drivers, pregnant women, or any party guests who choose not to drink alcohol. Although many drinks can be prepared without alcohol, some are especially important with underlined health benefits. They can be served frozen, fizzy, non-fizzy and cream-based.

I love Mocktails because they are an alternative to alcoholic drinks and allow everyone to enjoy the true essence of a celebratory occasion.

Mocktail and Me offers a variety of drinks ranging from sweet, zesty, earthy to fresh, featuring ingredients targeted help to boost your immune system and improve your overall health.

WHY MOCKTAILS?

Mocktails are as healthy as the ingredients you add into them. So it is advised to avoid artificial sugar, some fruits drinks and concentrates as they can be artificially flavored. Here are some great health benefits for mocktails:

Because the base is always a natural fruit drink gotten from juicing, it is an excellent alternative for fruit intake for when you are bored of eating raw fruits and vegetables

Mocktails are easy to make and inexpensive: You definitely don't need to be a bartender to create a good mocktail and they are typically ready within a timeframe of 15- 20mins.They are also an economical way to make good use of fruits.

No Hangovers: unlike a cocktail party, a mocktail party won't leave you hungover and miserable the next day.

They are hydrating, non-addictive and are packed with nutrients that are recommended to boost your gut health.

CHOOSING A JUICER OR A BLENDER

I am not an expert for sourcing the best juicers or blenders out there however, I have researched and concluded on some of the necessary questions to ask prior to purchasing one. As soon as you decide on the type of juicer to buy, the below questions would guide you when comparing to other brands:

What kind of produce do you plan to juice or blend? For example, you will need a **700 - 1000 watts in strength** to juice carrots, sugar cane on a daily basis, and a lower watt strength for fruits like oranges, watermelon and pineapple.

Is it easy to assemble and dissemble to clean? Choose a juicer that is easy to use on a daily respective to working it, using and putting it back together

Capacity? If you plan to juice for yourself, you will be just fine with a medium sized juicer. however, if you are juicing for your family, or plan to juice on a regular basis, then a large sized juicer will be needed.

Warranty? It is advised to ensure that your juicer comes with a written guarantee promising to repair or replace if necessary within a time period of 6 months to a year. **Cost?** I am afraid to say that you will need to invest in a durable juicer priced between the range of 60 - 100 dollars or above if you wish. Don't break your bank account trying to equate quality for price.

HEALTH BENEFITS OF RECOMMENDED FRUITS

Eating fruits and vegetables are part of an overall healthy diet and have proven to reduce the risk of certain chronic diseases. Overall, it is recommended to improve on your daily fruit intake in order to promote a healthy living standard. Here are few benefits of some of the fruits that are used in the recipes:

Orange - they are a good source of vitamin C, minerals and antioxidants. For this reason, they may lower the risk of cardiovascular disease and kidney stones.

Watermelon - contain a high level of lycopene which are very effective at protecting cells from damage . The extracts help to reduce hypertension and lower blood pressure.

Apple - may be good for your weightloss, linked to lower risk of diabetes and may contain compounds that can help fight asthma.

Carrot - particularly a good source of beta carotene, fiber, vitamin K1 and antioxidants. They are weight loss friendly and have been linked to lower cholesterol levels and improved vision.

Cucumber - low in calories and contain a good amount of water and soluble fiber, making them ideal for promoting hydration and aiding weight loss.

Pineapple - a good source of vitamin C and bromelain which helps to clear your sinus.

Mango- aids digestion, clears skin and promotes healthy gut.

SUGGESTED ADDITIVES

To enhance flavor and allow room for more health benefits, you can add additives such as aloe Vera, chlorella, flaxseed, hemp seed, probiotics and whey powder.

Below are some of the additives that have been added to some or all of the mocktails:

Ginger - the health benefits of ginger such as reducing gas and improving digestion earns it the role of a chief additive in these drinks

Mint leaf - it's cooling flavor, tendency to help cure headache and the beautiful finishing it adds to a drink are reasons it should not be left out of the party

Basil - it is believed that basil may help fight depression and promote skin health. what's a valid reason to leave them out?

Fresh thyme - would you believe that fresh thyme is packed with vitamin C and A? it is also great for combating a cold at the early stage.

Coconut water - helps with hydration and great for a good recovery after a workout. **Honey** - soothes cough and sore throat, improves memory and is a great substitute for artificial sugar.

Kombucha - potential source for probiotics, curbs hunger and reduces bloating. **Green tea** - the healthiest beverage on the planet. it is more than just a liquid **Raw sugar** - This is mostly used to rim the serving glass for aesthetic purposes. it can be optional if you choose.

MOCKTAILS AND WEIGHT LOSS

The benefits to drinking select mocktails are endless however, they are neither the panacea to every health problems nor do they guarantee weight loss by itself (because there is no such term as "fat burning juice"). Using this as an aid for weight loss will require extra hard work and dedication just like any other lifestyle. If you are willing to be work out and eat right, it can certainly help you to lose weight. Replacing processed food with freshly squeezed drinks will offer a significant reduction in calories. Without an elaborate discussion on weight loss, it is not rocket science to know that the key to losing weight is to create a calorie deficit so your body burns up stored fat for energy. This doesn't translate to eating below the expected daily calories which your body needs to maintain required functions.

These drinks may help you lose weight by flushing out excess toxins from your body and increasing nutrient intake. Another benefit to weight loss is that some of these fruits are so high in dietary fiber which might help to decrease your appetite and curb cravings. If you are trying to not exceed the expected daily calorie count,these drinks will help keep you in check. In addition to these drinks and a healthy diet, you can also boost your weight loss by adopting an active lifestyle.

Please research more information to help with your weight loss as this is not an exhaustive recommendation.

EVERYDAY MOCKTAILS

On days when you feel as though water is not enough, these category of Mocktails guarantee a refreshing combination of both water and delicious fruits.

Q'S VIBE - MY FAVORITE!

Q's Vibe is not just a drink but a reminder that each day is a gift of beauty, and should be appreciated with this colorful and refreshing mix.

Course: Drinks . Prep Time: 20mins. Serving: 2 - 3 drinks

INGREDIENTS:

- 2 cups watermelon balls

- ½ cup blackberry 2 - 3 mint leaves

- ½ cup mango and any preferred fruit

- ½ cup simple honey syrup (raw honey dissolved in lukewarm water)

- 2 cups coconut water or kombucha

- ¼ cup fresh ginger and lemon liquid

PREPARATION:

Using a melon baller, scoop 2 cups water melon balls and set aside

Into a blender, add ¾ cup water to thumb-size ginger and one peeled lemon. blend and strain

In a pitcher or water melon bowl, combine all the above ingredients and allow to sit for 10mins

Add crushed ice into a serving glass, using a serving ladle - scoop the drink into a cup, garnish with mint and enjoy!

MOCK O'CLOCK

If there's a drink synonymous to an alarm clock, this will be my recommendation. The only difference is you wake up with excitement!

Course: Drinks . Prep Time: 20mins. Serving: 2 -3 drinks

INGREDIENTS:

- 3 cups mix of red and black grapes 2 cups blackberry

- ¼ peeled lemon or lime 2-3 mint leaves

- ¼ cup simple honey syrup (honey dissolved in lukewarm water)

- ¼ cup fresh ginger

- 2 cups water

PREPARATION:

Blend all the above listed ingredients and strain

Transfer into a pitcher and fill with ice

14

Serve in a clean glass

Garnish with mint and enjoy!

NATURE'S GIFT

Are you into nature? If yes, then get a cup and pretend it's your canvas - except that this time you won't be hanging it.

Course: Drinks . Prep Time: 20mins. Serving: 2 -3 drinks

INGREDIENTS:

- 2 cups cucumber

- 1 cup celery

- 3 sprigs mint leaf

- ½ peeled lime

- 3 tbsp. honey, dissolved in half cup warm water

- ¼ cup fresh ginger 1 jalapeno

- 3 cups water or coconut water

PREPARATION:

Blend all the above listed ingredients and strain

Transfer into a pitcher and add ice

Serve in a clean glass

Garnish with mint, jalapeno and enjoy!

SHAKE IT ALL OFF

After meeting deadlines and smashing daily tasks, I am pretty sure you would want to SHAKE IT ALL OFF with a drink. Now let's do it!

Course: Drinks . Prep Time: 20mins. Serving: 3-4 drinks

INGREDIENTS:

- Half watermelon

- 1 cup raspberry, 1 tbsp raw sugar

- 1 sprig mint leaf

- ½ peeled lemon

- ¼ cup fresh ginger

- Watermelon balls togarnish

PREPARATION:

Feed watermelon chunks, lemon, ginger, mint leaf into the juicer, extract the juice and transfer into a pitcher

Combine a cup raspberry, 1 tbsp. raw sugar, mash in a clean ramekin and strain for a smoother texture

Add ice into a glass and pour the watermelon mix, top with raspberry syrup and stir

Garnish with mint leaf, 2-3 watermelon balls and enjoy!

SUNRISE

The rising of the sun signifies a new dawn filled with daily goals and I guarantee that this mocktail is willing to help you smash them all. Now let's go!

Course: Drinks . Prep Time: 20mins. Serving: 2 - 3 drinks

INGREDIENTS:

- 3 cups sweet orange chunks

- 1 cup raspberry

- 1 lemon

- 2 tbsp. raw sugar

- 3 sprigs mint leaf or basil to garnish

PREPARATION:

Feed orange and lemon chunks into the juicer, extract and transfer into a pitcher

Combine a cup raspberry, 2 tbsp. raw sugar, mash in a clean ramekin and strain for a smoother texture

Add ice into a glass and pour the orange and lemon juice, top with raspberry syrup and stir

Garnish with mint leaf and enjoy!

DREAMY MOCKTAILS

Dreamy Mocktails was created with an intention to help you unwind, get a good sleep and refuel for the next day. The combination in these drinks are intentional, so get to the kitchen and encounter a rejuvenating experience.

A NIGHT- IN

This is for all my ladies who like to get together on the weekend for a glass of red wine and lots of gossip! A NIGHT-IN is what you need to sit back and have a deserved girl chat.

Course: Drinks . Prep Time: 20mins. Serving: 2 - 3 drinks

INGREDIENTS:

- 5 - 6 cups ripe pineapple chunks

- ½ cup raw honey dissolved in warm water

- 4 cups cucumber chunks, ¼ cup fresh ginger

- 3 green apple, 1 lemon cut in chunks

- 2 cups spinach

PREPARATION:

Feed pineapple and lemon chunks into the juicer, extract and transfer into a pitcher

Add honey syrup and stir untilcombined

Feed cucumber, 3 green apples, ginger and spinach into the juicer, and extract

Add ice into a glass and pour green juice, top with pineapple juice and stir Garnish with cucumber strip and enjoy!

MOCKTALE

With MOCKTALE, you'd have the best evening chatting with your friends and laughing to good memories - imagine that without being drunk.

Course: Drinks . Prep Time: 20mins. Serving: 2 - 3 drinks

INGREDIENTS:

- 5 cups ripe orange chunks

- ½ cup raw honey dissolved in warm water

- 4 cups large carrot chunks

- ¼ cup fresh ginger

- 1 lemon cut in chunks

PREPARATION:

Feed orange and lemon chunks into the juicer, extract and transfer into a pitcher

Add honey syrup and stir until combined

Feed carrot chunks into the juicer, extract and set aside

Add ice into a glass and pour carrot juice, top with orange-lemon juice and stir

Garnish with mint leaf and enjoy!

PARTY MOCKTAILS

I thought of FINESSE in a cup and created these visually appealing drinks to entice your guests and add a touch of elegance to your occasion.

VITAME

Believing that self love is also reflected in the way you take care of your body, vitame promises to ensure your daily dose of vitamins. It is refreshing!

Course: Drinks . Prep Time: 20mins. Serving: 2 - 3 drinks

INGREDIENTS:

- 2 cups grape fruit chunks

- 2 cups orange chunks

- 2 cups tangerine, 1 cup blood orange (optional)

- 1 cup lemon chunks

- ½ cup raw honey dissolved in warm water

- ¼ cup fresh ginger

- 2-3 sprigs mint leaf

PREPARATION:

Feed grape, orange, tangerine, blood orange, ginger and lemon chunks into the juicer, extract and transfer into a pitcher

Add honey syrup and stir until combined

Add ice into a glass and pour citrus juice and stir

Garnish with mint leaf and enjoy!

Q'S ISLAND

Once you pour a glass of Q'S ISLAND, you'd ask for a tuneful Afropop. That awesome pair is an anecdote of who I am - a music and mango lover who enjoys dancing anywhere.

Course: Drinks . Prep Time: 20mins. Serving: 1 - 2 drinks

INGREDIENTS:

- 2 cups frozen or fresh mango

- 4 tbsp. honey dissolved in warm water

- 2 cups sweet oranges chunks

- ¼ cup fresh ginger

- 3 sprigs basil leaf to garnish

PREPARATION:

Feed ginger and orange chunks into the juicer, extract and transfer into a pitcher

Blend the mango into a puree and set aside

Pour the orange drink half way into each glass

Add pureed mango and coconut water to fill up each glass

Stir and add ice if necessary

Garnish with basil and enjoy!

IT'S ALL YOU

Just as the name implies, you are in total control of the added fruits. "ITS ALL YOU" is intended to give priority to your guest's choice. Everyone loves to feel important and valued.

Course: Drinks . Prep Time: 20mins. Serving: 2 - 3 drinks

INGREDIENTS:

- 2 cups any fruit of your choice

- 2 tbsp. honey dissolved in warm water

- 2 cups sugar cane juice or fresh coconut water

- 3 sprigs mint leaf to garnish

PREPARATION:

Pour the honey mix, sugar cane juice or fresh coconut water into a pitcher and stir

Add any fruit of your choice and sprigs of mint leaf

Gently stir again, refrigerate and allow to rest for 10 - 15mins

32

Serve in a clean glass

Garnish with mint leaf and enjoy!

BONUS - BEDTIME DETOX

Our bodies naturally detoxify everyday through the colon, liver and kidney. However, a little help is not a bad idea. To detox simply means to get rid of your body toxins, thereby improving overall health.

HERB-CITRUS CLEANSE (CAN LAST UP TO A WEEK REFRIGERATED)

As a creative food enthusiast, I am always searching for new methods to incorporate into my recipes and herbs always transcend. These leaves - basil, mint, thyme, rosemary, sage, cilantro and oregano - not only add enticing aroma, fresh flavor and green color to food, but also have an outstanding health benefits.

Adding fruits, aromatics, tea and honey (all natural ingredients) would only combine a plethora of beneficial components into a cup. This **HERB-CITRUS** detox acts as a relaxant before going to bed - which means you get enough sleep and wake up feeling energetic. It also helps to boost digestion, reduce gas & bloating and fights bad breath.

Warning: This detox tea is not intended to replace a medication or treat any medical condition. Consult your doctor if you are pregnant or breastfeeding. Ensure you are not allergic to any of the above mentioned ingredients before preparing this tea.

INGREDIENTS:

- 2 - 3 sprigs of basil, fresh thyme + mint

- 2 - 3 tbsp. honey

- 2 ginger coins

- 1 cup orange, tangerine

- 1 peeled lemon

- 1/2 cup sweet mango - optional

- Mint or preferred tea

PREPARATION:

Pour all ingredients into a sauce pan, add 2 - 3 cups of water and bring to a boil for 10 - 12mins

Allow to cool, strain and pour into a pitcher

Serve warm and enjoy

FUN FACTS

Did you know mint is a symbol of hospitality and wisdom?

Did you know raw beet is 88% water, 10% carbs & 1% fat?

Did you know that ginger oil can be used for perfume?

Did you know that the heaviest watermelon weighs 159kg?

Did you know that each blackberry flower is about 2-3 cm?

Did you know that raspberries represented kindness in early Christian artwork?

Did you know that a carrot everyday reduces the risk of stroke by 68%?

Did you know that February 6th is National Frozen Yogurt Day?

Did you know that peach is a Chinese symbol of longevity?

Did you know that some mango specimen can live up to 300 years and still bear fruits?

DISCLAIMER

All suggested Mocktails are not intended to replace a medication or treat any medical condition

Please consult your doctor if you are pregnant or breastfeeding

Ensure you are not allergic to any of the fruits before preparing any of these Mocktails

In any case where you notice any changes in your body, please stop and consult a medical professional

All information in this book is provided in good faith however, I am not a representation of a medical practitioner or a provider of any form of medical recommendations.

ACKNOWLEDGMENT

I cannot express enough thanks to God Almighty who revealed this idea and gave me the strength to make it a reality. To my family whose moral support played a big role in this journey, the graphic designer, Lilian Orukwo, my wonderful and supportive friends, and my foodies, you all have been a great motivator, and this wouldn't be possible without your help.

To you Nkemka V. Ozonma, thank you so much for everything! I am eternally grateful.

To my Late Father, Mr. Godson, Odimegwu, it is assuring to see that your legacy will continue to live on. Thank you for partly blessing me with the gift of culinary expertise.

Finally, to my caring, loving, and supportive Mom, Veronica: my sincere gratitude. Your prayers and encouragement when the times got rough are much appreciated. It is a great feeling knowing that I have and will always have you. I dedicate this book to you as a symbol of my appreciation for all that you have sacrificed for my siblings and I. You are the strongest woman I know, and words cannot describe how much I love you. My heartfelt thanks!

ABOUT THE AUTHOR

Queeneth Odimegwu, a Nigerian born personal Chef who is the lead digital content creator behind one of the fastest growing food biogs (Dishes_By_Q) on lnstagram. Queeneth believes she would connect the world through her exceptional and pioneering culinary experience.

Alongside developing recipes for food and drinks, she has worked as a Quality Assurance Analyst at PriceWaterhouseCoopers, Software Testing Analyst at Jackson National Life and currently a Project Management Coordinator at The World Bank.

Queeneth has built a great reputation in corporate America, but her favorite job is spending time in the kitchen after work, and all day during the weekends- developing or modifying recipes. To emphasize how happy, she can be in the kitchen, Queeneth enjoys dancing while cooking as she believes that good food should be paired with great music.

You can connect with Queeneth on lnstagram (Dishes_By_Q) where you can sign up to receive notifications of her daily intriguing video recipes.

GLOSSARY

B

Basil - culinary herb of the family Lamiaceeae

Bring to a boil - to heat a liquid until it begins to bubble and steam

C

Chop - to cut food into bite-sized pieces

Chunk- a thick solid piece of something

Cinnamon - an aromatic spice made from the peeled, dried and rolled bark of a Southeast Asian tree

F

Flavored - having been given a particular taste by the addition of a flavoring

G

Garnish - decorate or embellish food

Ginger coin - cut ginger into the shape of a coin

J

Jalapeno - a very hot chili pepper used in Mexican-style cooking

M

Melon baller - a spoonlike utensil for cutting ball-shaped pieces from the pulp of a fruit

Mint leaf - an herb with fresh tasting leaves

Mocktail - a nonalcoholic drink consisting of various ingredients (such as juice, herbs and sparkling water)

P

Pitcher - a large container with a handle and a lip, used for holding and pouring liquids

S

Serving ladle - a large spoon with a deep bowl for scooping andserving liquids

Sparkling water - effervescent beverage artificially charged with carbon dioxide

Sprig - a small stem bearing leaves or flowers taken from a plant

Strain - pour a liquid through a perforated material in order to separate out solid matter

Strainer - a perforated device used for straining liquids

Stir move or cause to move slightly

Queeneth Odimegwu

"THERE'S A DRINK FOR EVERYONE"

-QUEENETH ODIMEGWU

Made in the USA
Coppell, TX
27 October 2020